The Brumback Library

PRESENTED BY:

The Kiwanis Club
of
Van Wert

The Hen Can't Help It
A First Look at the Life Cycle of a Chicken

First Look:
Science

by Sam Godwin
illustrated by Simone Abel

Thanks to our reading adviser:

Susan Kesselring, M.A., Literacy Educator
Rosemount-Apple Valley-Eagan (Minnesota) School District

PICTURE WINDOW BOOKS
Minneapolis, Minnesota

First American edition published in 2005 by
Picture Window Books
5115 Excelsior Boulevard
Suite 232
Minneapolis, MN 55416
877-845-8392
www.picturewindowbooks.com

First Published in Great Britain in 2001 by Hodder Wayland
Hodder Children's Books
A division of Hodder Headline Limited
338 Euston Road
London NW1 3BH

Printed in the United States of America.

Library of Congress Cataloging-in-Publication Data
Godwin, Sam.
The hen can't help it : a first look at the life cycle of a chicken /
by Sam Godwin ; illustrated by Simone Abel.
p. cm.—(First look : science)
ISBN 1-4048-0653-9 (hardcover)
1.Chickens—Life cycles—Juvenile literature. I. Abel, Simone.
II. Title. III. Series.
SF487.5.G64 2004
636.5—dc22
2004007319

To Jake Pirotta – SG
To Pamela Hodgson – SA

3

A hen sits quietly on her nest. She looks fast asleep,

4

raises her tail, and lays an egg!

Then the hen walks around to stretch her legs.

The rooster brings her something to eat.

Here you are, darling. Your favorite!

Yuck!

9

When the hen has enough eggs in her nest,

Inside each egg, a baby chicken is growing.

At first, it is just a tiny speck.

Then the chick starts to grow

14

The chick is growing legs and wings and a tail. It has feathers, too.

bigger and bigger.

Wow!

Are you OK, Hen? You've been sitting there for three whole weeks.

I'm a bit stiff, dear.

The chick also grows a sharp tip on its beak.

16

17

19

I bet they're hungry.

At last, the chicks have hatched.

No, they have just eaten up the last of the egg yolk.

They are wet and tired from all that tapping.

21

The chicks hide under their mother's wings.

My little chicks—
they're all so
eggstraordinary!

But soon they are dry and ready to play.

run, and fly up to a perch.

Soon the chicks grow into hens and roosters.

The Chicken Life Cycle

1 A grown-up hen lays some eggs in a nest. She sits on them to keep them warm.

6 Five months after they hatched, the chicks have become grown-up hens and roosters.

5 The chicks begin to explore the world around them.

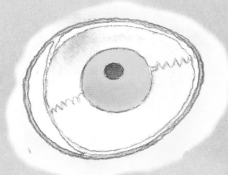

  2 Inside each egg, a tiny chick begins to grow.

  3 After three weeks, the chicks hatch.

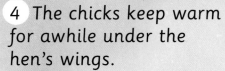 4 The chicks keep warm for awhile under the hen's wings.

Useful Words

Chick
A young chicken.

Hatch
To come out of an egg.

Hen
A female adult chicken.

Nest
The home of some birds, insects, or other animals.
Some creatures are born in the nest.

Perch
A place, such as a bar or a branch, for
a bird to rest.

Rooster
A male adult chicken.

Yolk
A yellow sack inside an egg, full of food
for the unhatched chick.

Fun Facts

- The most yolks ever found in one egg is nine.
- The largest chicken egg weighed almost 12 ounces (336 grams), which is the same as a can of soda.
- Some types of chickens can lay colored eggs, including blue and green.
- There are more chickens in the world than people.

To Learn More

At the Library

Roche, Hannah. *Have You Ever Seen a Chick Hatch?* New York: Zero to Ten, 1998.

Royston, Angela. *Life Cycle of a Chicken.* Des Plaines, Ill.: Heinemann Library, 1998.

Sklansky, Amy E. *Where Do Chicks Come From?* New York: HarperCollins, 2005.

On the Web

FactHound offers a safe, fun way to find Web sites related to this book. All of the sites on FactHound have been researched by our staff. *www.facthound.com*

1. Visit the FactHound home page.
2. Enter a search word related to this book, or type in this special code: 1404806539.
3. Click the FETCH IT button.

Your trusty FactHound will fetch the best Web sites for you!

Index

Look for all the books in this series: